LITTLE TIMMY THE PAINTED BUNTING

Thanks to the North family.

Thanks to my friend Channe Felton, who asked me to write a little story about the Painted Bunting. The poem herein developed out of that and inspired the illustrations.

Thanks to Kathleen Shields for her tireless work in bringing the book to completion and for adding the Bunting colors to the book cover title.

ISBN-13: 978-1-956581-60-7   Hardback

Acrylic Illustrations by: Michael P. Earney

ERIN GO BRAGH
Publishing

Canyon Lake, Texas
www.ErinGoBraghPublishing.com

**Pretty Mrs. Painted Bunting
is on a quest!**

**To find a place
to build her nest.**

(Low trees or shrubs
close to the ground,
where it won't be
too easily found.)

She had flown in from far, far away
just to arrive on this Spring day.

(Nearly a thousand miles or so,
that's a very long way, you know.)

Soon she picked what was the very best
and there she made her
baby Bunting nest.

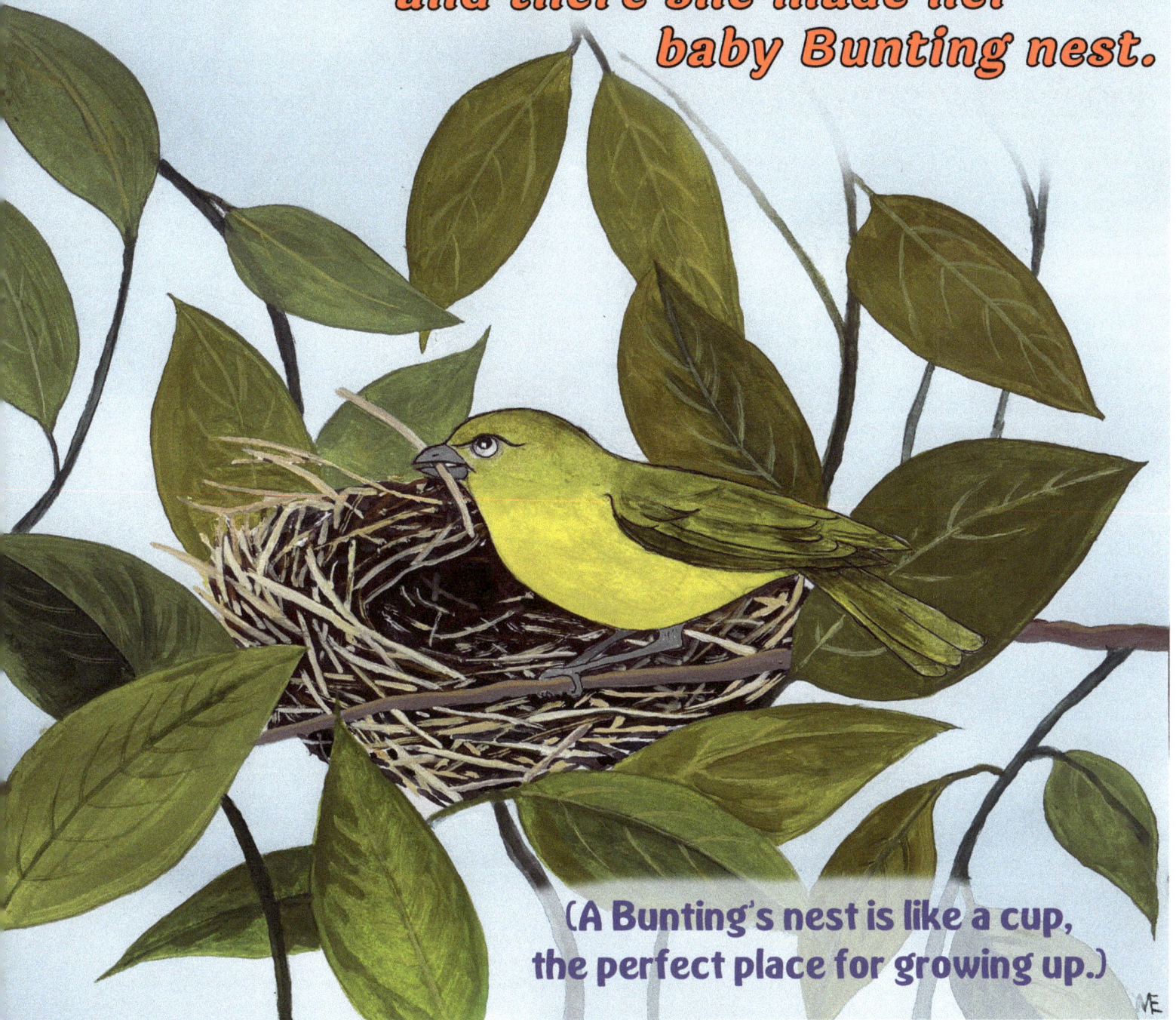

(A Bunting's nest is like a cup,
the perfect place for growing up.)

In that small nest she laid three eggs,
one was Charlotte's,
one was Tim's,
and one was Greg's.

(Five is what a Bunting lays at most,
but Mrs. Bunting didn't want to boast.)

Then Mrs. Cowbird came and laid another,
so Mrs. Bunting would become its mother.

(Cowbirds are such
awful pests,
they lay their eggs
in other's nests.)

The cowbird grew and moved around, pushing little Timmy to the ground.

(Cowbirds grow faster than the rest, and take up nearly half the nest!)

Alice lived on the farm nearby,
and saw that Timmy could not fly.

(See a sick bird on the ground?
Tell an adult what you found.)

Timmy was taken to that family farm, where he grew up, free from harm.

(Something you may not have heard, you must not keep a wild bird.)

Timmy is strong
no longer frail.

So this becomes
a happy tale.

(Cowbirds often throw
the stepmother's eggs
out of the nest.
Those Cowbirds, as I said,
can be a pest.)

We last saw Timmy as a juvenile,
to see him now
will make you smile.

(Look how
brightly colored
he is here,
now he's in his
second year!)

The End.

Little Timmy the Painted Bunting

Pretty Mrs. Painted Bunting is on a quest!
To find a place to build her nest.

She had flown in from far, far away
Just to arrive on this Spring day.

Soon she picked what was the very best
And there she made her baby Bunting nest.

In that small nest she laid three eggs,
One was Charlotte's, one was Tim's
and one was Greg's.

Then Mrs. Cowbird came and laid another,
So Mrs. Bunting would become its mother.

The cowbird grew and moved around,
Pushing little Timmy to the ground.

Alice lived on the farm nearby,
and saw that Timmy could not fly.

Timmy was taken to that family farm,
Where he grew up, free from harm.

Timmy is strong, no longer frail.
So this become a happy tale.

We last saw Timmy as a juvenile,
To see him now will make you smile.

Low trees or shrubs close to the ground,
Where it won't be too easily found.

Nearly a thousand miles or so,
That's a very long way, you know.

A Bunting's nest is like a cup,
The perfect place for growing up.

Five is what a Bunting lays at most.
But Mrs. Bunting didn't want to boast.

Cowbirds are such awful pests,
They lay their eggs in other's nests.

Cowbirds grow faster than the rest,
And take up nearly half the nest!

See a sick bird on the ground?
Tell an adult what you found.

Something you may not have heard
you must not keep a wild bird.

Cowbirds often throw the stepmother's eggs out of the nest.
Those Cowbirds, as I said, can be a pest.

Look how brightly colored he is here,
Now he's in his second year!

Michael P. Earney is a renowned fine arts painter and has been a commercial artist, ceramic sculptor, a potter, an award-winning documentary filmmaker and published author of numerous works.

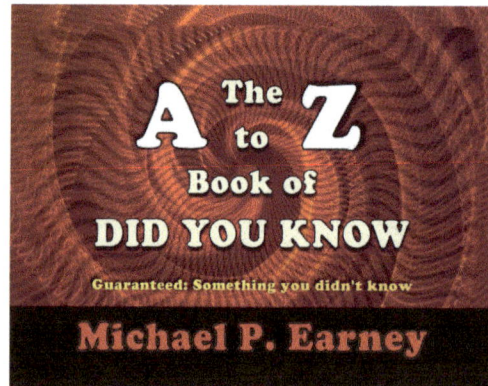

The A to Z
Book of
DID YOU KNOW
Guaranteed: Something you didn't know
Michael P. Earney

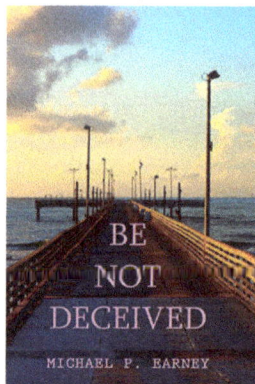

BE NOT DECEIVED
MICHAEL P. EARNEY

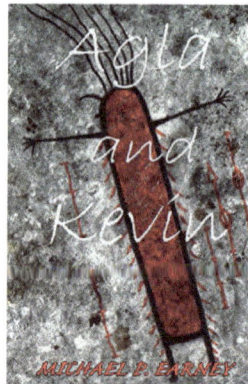

Agla and Kevin
MICHAEL P. EARNEY

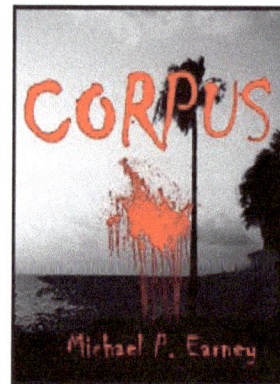

CORPUS
Michael P. Earney

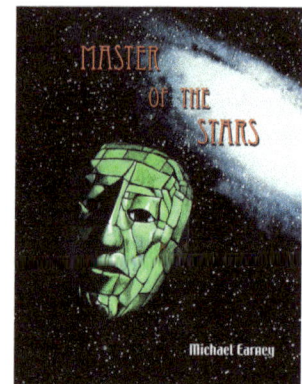

MASTER OF THE STARS
Michael Earney

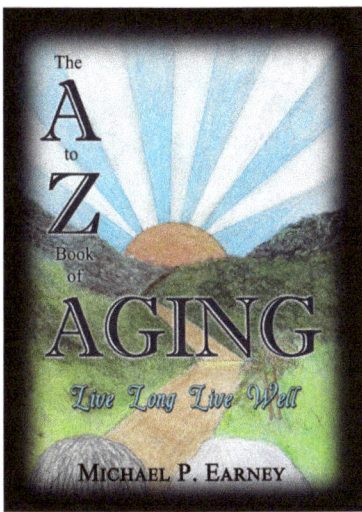
The A to Z Book of AGING
Live Long Live Well
Michael P. Earney

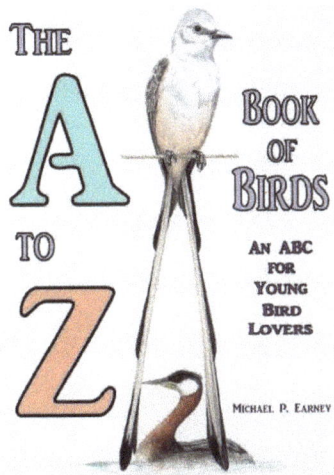
The A to Z Book of BIRDS
An ABC for Young Bird Lovers
Michael P. Earney

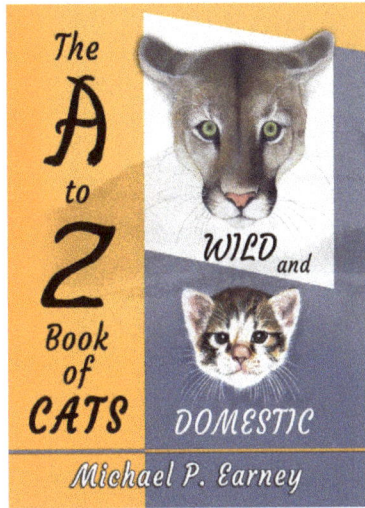
The A to Z Book of CATS
WILD and DOMESTIC
Michael P. Earney

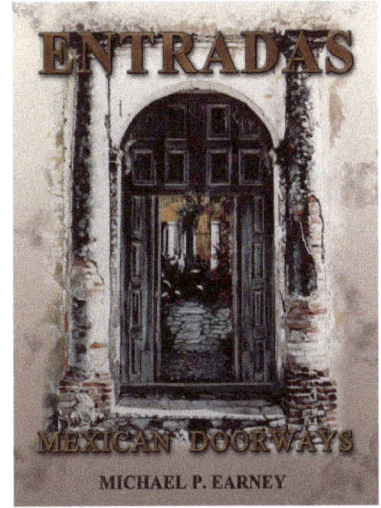
ENTRADAS
MEXICAN DOORWAYS
Michael P. Earney

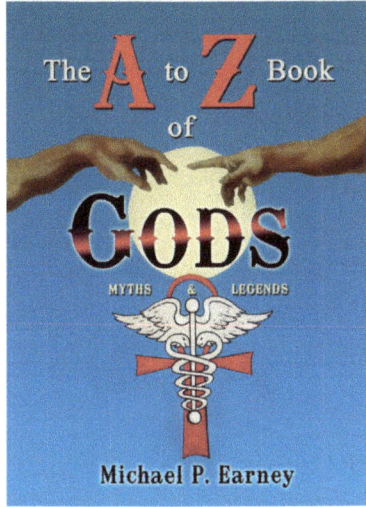
The A to Z Book of GODS
MYTHS & LEGENDS
Michael P. Earney

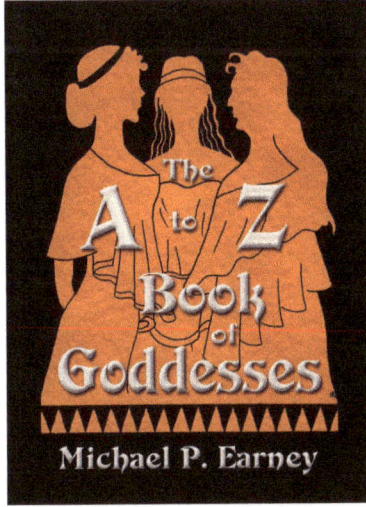
The A to Z Book of Goddesses
Michael P. Earney

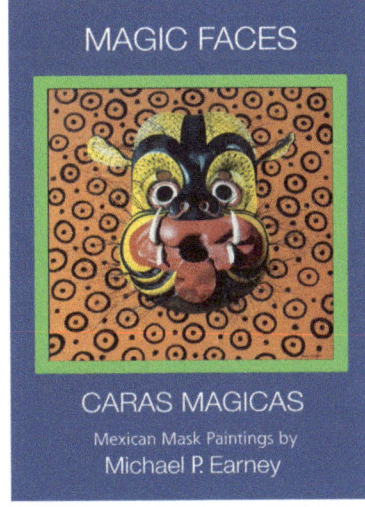
MAGIC FACES
CARAS MAGICAS
Mexican Mask Paintings by
Michael P. Earney

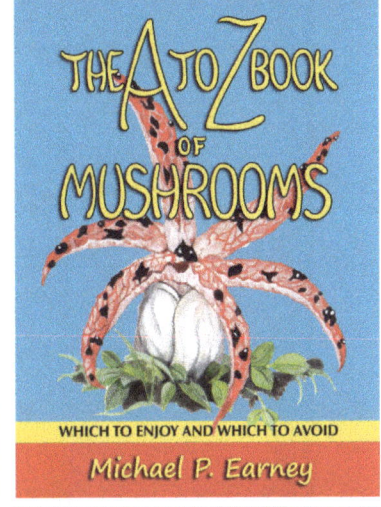
THE A TO Z BOOK OF MUSHROOMS
WHICH TO ENJOY AND WHICH TO AVOID
Michael P. Earney

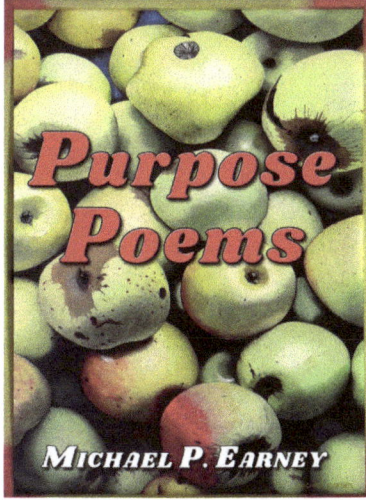
Purpose Poems
Michael P. Earney

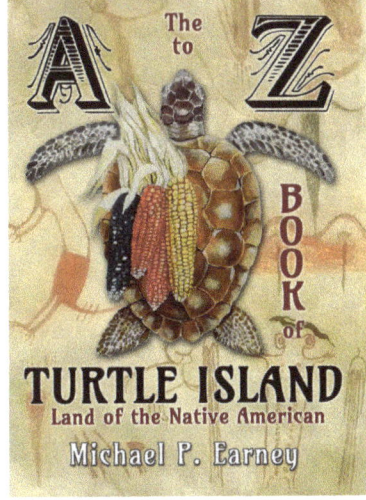
The A to Z Book of TURTLE ISLAND
Land of the Native American
Michael P. Earney

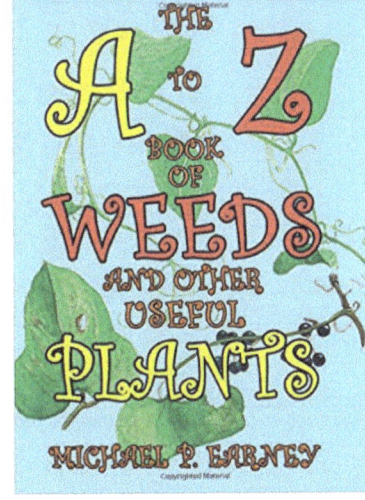
THE A to Z BOOK OF WEEDS AND OTHER USEFUL PLANTS
MICHAEL P. EARNEY

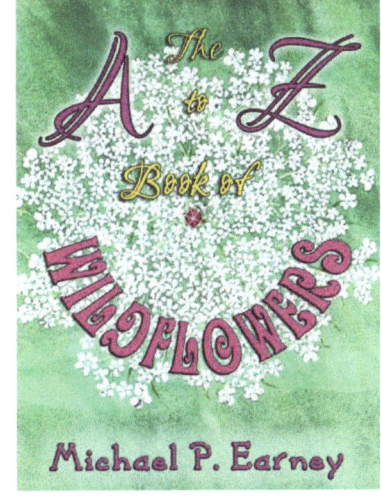
The A to Z Book of WILDFLOWERS
Michael P. Earney

ERIN GO BRAGH
Publishing

Erin Go Bragh Publishing publishes various genres of books for numerous authors. Their portfolio consists of a 1200-page Vietnamese to English Dictionary, Historical fiction, an award-winning children's educational series, multiple adult novels and memoirs, tween adventure stories, poetry as well as Christian Fiction for all ages.

Their objective is to promote literacy and education through reading and writing.

www.ErinGoBraghPublishing.com
Canyon Lake, Texas

www.ingramcontent.com/pod-product-compliance
Lightning Source LLC
Chambersburg PA
CBHW040850100426
42813CB00015B/2766